EXIT
THE
BODY

EXIT
THE
BODY

ESSAYS

HEATHER BARTEL

Published by Split/Lip Press
PO Box 27656
Ralston, NE 68127
www.splitlippress.com

ISBN: 978-1-952897-37-5

Cover and Book Design: David Wojciechowski
Cover Art: RawPixel
Editing: Lauren W. Westerfield

CONTENTS

For Kate. I am who I am because of you
and who I am because you're gone.

YET
THE PHANTOM
WAS PART OF
THE FLOWER

What follows in an illusion.
What follows is a dance.
A secret.
A dream.

Curiosity didn't kill the cat, it only prompted an upset stomach, strands of wet grass spewed onto the porch left to dry powder-yellow in pollen, and just like all the other messes I'll be the one to clean it up, or to ignore it, and pretend I am proving a point when in fact all I am doing is pretending to disappear. I wait for the mail to arrive and when none of what I collect is addressed to my name I begin to wonder.

My first fascination was Amelia Earhart—tethered ghost-sister, cross-generational friend. I didn't give a damn about aviation. I only cared that the truth of the end of her life was shaky, only cared about the chorus of words spread through every book: *woman, disappeared, died.* Most likely her bones were laid to rest somewhere deep in the ocean, lungs filled with enough water that fish could swim around in them, so much salt and wetness swallowed that her throat decided to never swallow again. Most likely the end was fast and simple, bang, rattle, spiral, crash, and there was never enough of a body left to find. There remains the chance, however, that Amelia went swimming, or landed on an island, or took her plane to another destination, fled the scene, changed her name. My admiration for her bloomed out of these seeds of possibility, out of a romantic notion: perhaps she had discovered how to become a ghost while she was still alive.

An illusion. A dance. A secret. A dream.
An echo a promise a misunderstanding an undoing a tearing apart an art
a prayer a scream.

Special Agent Dale Cooper and a woman who is or is not Laura Palmer, who looks like Laura but is alive into her forties, with another name in another town, are walking across the street, back from what had been, perhaps in another decade or another dimension, the Palmer house. The sky is dark, the street they are crossing is quiet and empty. They do not speak to one another until Cooper pauses, turns back to face the house and, bewildered, asks, *What year is this?* And for a moment Laura/Not-Laura stands still, as if thinking, as if searching, and then, suddenly, she screams, piercing, the blade of a knife carving out shape in the quiet, the sound of breaking glass. The lights on in the windows of the house looming behind them go black. *What year is this?* She screams. What year, and who is she, and which version of life has she dreamed?

Sanity is found at the centre of convulsion, where madness is scorched from the bisected soul.

I dream of finding a black feather and assume this must mean I am dying, another stray warning meant to symbolize the clock ticking closer to midnight, the ink fading, another reminder of my impending demise. When my head hurts I keep it to myself, call it a tumor, an aneurysm, prepare for the worst, accept it, go quiet and convince myself there is nothing left to hope for. Two days after the dream I find a feather in the yard, though this one is neither as black nor as crescent-shaped as

the one I had dreamed of; it is scrawny and matted from the rai/
days after that I find another, this time in the grass along the si.
a few blocks from home, and this one is straighter, lovelier, deep gray; 1
place it on a windowsill altar perpendicular to my desk, next to shards of
colored glass, amber and lavender, that I've found buried in the dirt—*I
must be getting closer.*

*An echo, the bones of a ghost, the dust and the honey and the song and the
throat, wrapped in plastic, a trick of the eye, an open window   an illusion   a
woman   a ghost.*

I am driving my grandfather's truck on a familiar road in Missouri, home
but not home, an impulsive trip ending this afternoon with a flight
back to Georgia, mustard-colored backpack carrying all I had needed
to bring. I am thinking disconnected thoughts and then I am thinking
nothing but in my head I am screaming, I am visualizing a woman's face,
my own face, screaming, I am hearing the scream, and I look up and do
not recognize the houses do not recognize the landscape do not recognize even the steering wheel, I am not screaming, am I. I pull over in
the parking lot of an old barn-turned-theater, and as I breathe into the
return to reality of self/body/situation, I shake from the disorientation
of the removal from it, the question of *how did I get here* less frightening
than the knowledge that *I* have been *here* all along.

Could be anywhere. Shhhh. (She screams.)

What David Lynch's oeuvre teaches us: everything is an illusion. And
even—especially—when we wake up, we catch ourselves questioning
how much of the night was a dream. His work is best digested when left
partially unchewed, meant to remain on the tongue without being able
to determine just why, exactly, one recognizes the taste. Lynch reckons
with the unfamiliar familiar of parallel universes, alternate realities, psy-
chic visions, dreams; perhaps he does not reckon so much as he manip-
ulates, dissects, unravels.

*Illusion shapes and shelters us, as necessary as oxygen and water. Illusions won't
die, they are not delusions, and seem part of a human being's hard-wiring.*

Audrey Horne at the Roadhouse, revisiting an old haunt, dances the
way she did twenty-five years ago in her red high-heeled shoes, dances,
eyes closed, to the same music she used to dance to—*I love this music,*

isn't it too dreamy? Now, when she dances it does feel dreamlike, her first moment of peace in too long, and it makes me wonder if her dancing had always been a drift into dream, a drift toward the edges of reality or a removal from it completely. When the music stops and the club goes sour—a yell, a crash, a fight breaks out, bodies once again fill the dance floor—she runs to her companion, pleading, *get me out of here.* Get me out of here—this is the last thing she says before the scene cuts to Audrey looking in a mirror in a white-walled room, her reflection shocked, horrified, profoundly confused—where is she now and where was she then? When she says, *get me out of here*, does she mean the Roadhouse, the dream, the dance—or does she mean the version of her life we see her in in that final moment, staring broken into the mirror? The episode ends as she is touching her face, on the verge of releasing a scream: *get me out of here.* Bright white shock cuts to emptiness, finality, black.

A body   an echo   an illusion   a dream   a ghost   a ghost   a ghost
a ghost.

I dream a series of attempted home invasions, all occurring in what would be considered real time, the time in which my body is sleeping, and the place, this bed, the yellow blanket, the streetlight just beyond the window, and the stop sign, the sound of wind or car engine or dog barking or rain. What I know is there in the darkness—the bed, the ceiling fan, the walls, the window—is there, too, behind my closed eyes. In every vision, someone is coming toward the bedroom window; in every version, their approach is sinister. In one of the dreams the wind is scattering leaves and pieces of trash around the yard, funneling its own warning of all that could be coming to call for me. I wake up convinced I should be sleeping with the yellow-handled kitchen knife we don't use tucked into my nightstand drawer, now that my partner leaves for work in the hours of the morning most people still consider night; I wake with a plan to call a trusted male co-worker should anything happen to me, establishing a plan that feels rational, a plan for protection. My partner tells me if I keep a knife in my nightstand, he will no longer sleep with me, because we are both unreliable in our unconscious states, too much venom and agitation stirred up in dreams, edging us into awakened confusions. I get up to check that the door is locked every morning after he leaves.

I wonder, if Amelia's plane did crash after all, if it plummeted downward from sky to sea-blue, I wonder if the engine crackled and roared, if she knew what was coming, if she tried to fight for more breath, if she considered an exit strategy—jumping, riding some piece of busted aircraft miles to the nearest shore—or if instead she leaned into the current, arched her back with the dive, I wonder if she closed her eyes or if she watched the water coming. I wonder, did she take in all the air she could and in that final moment did she scream?

You are not dead, although you were dead. The girl who died. And was resurrected. Children. Witches. Magic. Symbols. Remember the illogic of fantasy.

The greatest trick of "Mulholland Drive": the illusion of illusion. The parallels: Diane as Betty, Rita in a blond wig to look like Diane, faces pressed together as if against a reflection, watching as a woman singing collapses, the song continues after she's dragged away, voice with no body, *llorando por tu amor. An illusion.* The performance is the illusion of both a body and what exists beyond it. The song exists beyond the woman; the song does not need the woman to sing it in order to exist. She is a vessel, a showpiece, a dream. The experience is like looking into a mirror and not seeing anyone there.

An art, a becoming, trapped in frames on the wall.
Tomorrow, tomorrow, no such thing.
An illusion   a mystery   a dream.

I get distracted one morning taking notes on "Mulholland Drive," write out the stages of death in my journal instead: *pallor mortis, algor mortis, rigor mortis, livor mortis, putrefaction, decomposition, skeletonization, fossilization*. Often, later, I will begin to misread the word *putrefy* as *purify*.

What I am attempting to discern is a balance between woman and ghost, the distinction these Lynchian women are searching for when they scream, the move toward an acceptance of a reality, whether this reality winds up being physical, actual, or contained within a mirror or dream, my face when I see it and notice my hair, is, in fact, red. A reflection shows what is tangible though the reflection itself is not; a woman bleeds into the experience of another, dizzies herself in the early morning hours asking, *Am I real? Am I alive?* It is the possibility of otherness, of disappearing into a dream or going to ghost, that the transformation could occur without our compliance or even without our noticing—this possibility is what haunts me when I see these women scream, when I am the one screaming, when all I can see behind my eyes is white and

I do not recognize what lies in front of me, what should be irrevocable, familiar, concrete.

Amelia, too, coming in over the radio: *Am I real? Am I alive?* All that is heard at the other end is static, perhaps, the roar of the ocean, the waves cloaking her story in silence.

The dead wear roses, wrapped in plastic, wrapped in smoke, and the moon grows full, and her hair goes red   a dream   a secret.

No such thing.

The mirror is feminine, aligned with the moon. A reflection is magic, that which is illuminated at night. She whispers in the darkness, this other, the one who haunts me, the one whose hair is red even though I cannot recognize this fire when I see her in the mirror. I am looking because I am afraid of not seeing. I am looking because the more I keep looking, the more I continue to find. We rinse and repeat as we wake, from blackness to blue, splash the face with cool water over the sink, fleck the mirror with the wetness, good morning, I see you, she says, *there you are*, she stands and she feels her face, my face, as it prepares to turn toward the light of the day, the sun, *good morning*, and at night, *be seeing you again, sweet dreams*. The phantom; the flower. The unwavering parallels: she is/she isn't, asleep/awake, Laura/Not-Laura, woman/ghost, disappeared/died, mirror/moon. I concentrate on my reflection and if I am awake or asleep it is unclear and she begins to blur, the faucet drips out black feathers, *see you soon*.

THE KNIFE
SPEAKS

a tarot reading performed with Sylvia Plath and a shot of whiskey

I. THE FOOL

We travel. Free and whole and unalarmed until sideswiped by the con-
sequences of possibility: expectation, revelation, vertigo. The stepping
over the edge before realizing the edge was there. The failure to heed
any warning, body in the sun, unaware of itself.

The telephone rings, it has something to say. The telephone rings, almost something living, an almost connection, illuminated phantom until the screen goes black. A mirror in my pocket: I can find my face in it.
But before a phone was a mirror, it came in parts. There used to be two
halves: the piece plugged into the wall and the part we held onto, han-
dle-shaped, in the hand and to the ear and the mouth, we cradled it, we
called it the receiver. Giving and receiving, these two halves: a process
like splitting the brain into left and right. Still the same brain but still
no one can see it. Still the same mirror but whose face is mine—I cannot
hang up this mirror anymore in a way that makes noise, cannot slam the

phone down can only slide a finger across the glass, let it go black.

A knife, too, has a handle to hold onto.

A knife carves its words into surfaces—tree bark, plaster, skin. Words appear, too, on the surface of the phone I keep sometimes in my pocket, the pocket where some people also keep knives folded, waiting to flick open, to slash, to strike. The message is the same every time: keep reading. The tarot cards say it too. A rearrangement of images but still the same story. The game is discovering which page we will start with this time.

Today it is a rearrangement of the same words: *today, she is.*

II. QUEEN OF SWORDS

I think I might be Sylvia Plath reincarnate. I study her features in the mirror. That I am her double is unremarkable: we all have a shadow, even at night. In the cards I am The Emperor, Aries; my moon The Devil, Capricorn; my self a shadow, the shadow of chaos, the chaos internal of the unforgiving self. I am a wildfire; I am scorched earth. I am Sylvia and she was ruled by Death. My eyes are gray but hers are grayer. Features go unshaped: when I am her, a nose is just a nose. I watch her face as I touch myself and I want to make her cum, know I am making her come, finger slipped inside, hot, pulsing, she is coming now, we are coming, we are coming together. We finish. She grins at me, we grin at each other, vibrating, red flush, the mirror a cold violence, the lover to lean into. I press my forehead against hers and feel the fever, see the fog spread with my breath, I touch the glass with the tip of my tongue and she receives it. She gives me her ear and I take, share the message through our secret game of telephone: *I want to spend my life with you* becomes I want to spin my life with you I want to spin my life untrue I want to spin a web or two I want to be a spider I want to spy on her I want to lie beside her I want to die beside her I want to die.

This dark thing that sleeps in me, I guess you could say I've a call. I know the bottom, oh, you strange girl—how you lie and cry after

what long ago hurt.

III. SIX OF CUPS

I wish I was the kind of person who found satisfaction in screaming. Instead of screaming I think about space. In space I hear there is no sound, no echo within the vacuum, unlike the roar behind the darkness when my eyelids fall shut. I wonder if in space I could even hear my own heartbeat. I wonder if I could even see my own breath. I hear space is cold, but so is the mirror. So is the blade of a knife, smooth and sharp, it's velvet, it's crystal, it's ice. Sylvia and I are both looking. Or if I am her, I am history repeating, the woven pattern, to be trapped within and broken through, strands of infinity left sticking in my hair, echoes of screams that were released centuries ago still piercing the quiet and each one is a reminder I've encountered the truth: neither knife nor phone is mirror. A phone is only a phone and a knife is only a knife and I am the only one speaking, I am the one who is speaking, I am the one in the mirror, I'm sad, I'm sad.

Another misunderstanding: *I am a disaster* becomes *don't look at me*.

I'll scream but the noise of it will not mean anything, will not translate to anything other than sound. I'll scream but only as long as I am breathing, and the echo of my emptiness will drift onward into space.

The truth is I don't want to be myself today.

Death is the only story I know, my body the process.

IV. THE MOON

Awareness has neither a center nor boundaries. Awareness is a house at night with the lights turned off, awareness is a mirror, there is always a mirror, there is always a mirror and I see from both sides. Every choice is an illusion and with each choice I risk an opening, like a star that punctures the night. A star is a shaped thing and it is a word, when it's written; a word is a voice is a light. I am her echo. The reflection of my face is never enough. I look again and return to the beginning, an offering: *you choose now, you choose*. But it is unclear when the beginning ends and the body becomes itself, the one doing the choosing rather than receiving the suggestion. A body does not choose to come into being, a mind does not choose the body it inhabits, and we do not choose to be born but then here we are, and here is the mirror reminding us we are seen. Here is the mirror, offering me a face I don't recognize as mine. Here is the mirror, saying *oh you strange girl*. Here is the mirror, saying *now you choose*.

I skirt around the subject by stepping out of the frame. Instead of unplugging my phone from the wall, instead of yanking, I slide my finger across the screen to turn it off. The transformation is as satisfying as stillness becoming stillness. The cold, dead rock of the moon offers the possibility of renewal when it appears in blackness, when the moon goes new, dark enough to see myself by—there goes my shadow, she's walking at night.

If I can reconstruct my mind to make sense of its calamity, if I can reinvent the mirror as that which reflects my body rather than that which deceives, if I can readapt to a knife in the kitchen as being only a knife,

if I can close my eyes without wanting to scream—
I might stand a chance.
Or if I stand before the glass again and then lean toward it, just a little
bit closer, if I lean in and catch her eye again and see that it's my eye and
we are the same—to   die   beside   her.
She winks at me.
She offers a beginning.

Now, you choose.

LETTERS TO
A LIVING
GHOST

Dear ghost sister, the ice is cold on my teeth—the nerve of these nerve-endings, preserving the life of me. Dear ghost sister, I am digging my thumbnails into my gums again. Dear ghost sister, you say you are not afraid, but I am still afraid of losing, I am still not ready to give up, I am still not ready for the wreckage of losing again, I am still. Dear ghost sister, a line to you becomes a paragraph, a wall of water, a heavy fog on the highway, the mountains that form the letters of your name. Dear ghost sister, are you still breathing? Dear ghost sister, I finally had a dream of her again last night, I hadn't seen her in such a long time, and it's been five years since she's eaten a plum. Dear ghost sister, I drew the Death card from my Tarot deck. Dear ghost sister, my gums are bleeding. Dear ghost sister, your handwriting is so small—how is it that you can be so illuminated in my memory and still bury yourself within this mound of leaves? Dear ghost sister, I hear your voice, too. I feel your hand reaching across the table, see the tears in your eyes as they are spilling from my throat. Dear ghost sister, my mailbox is empty. Dear ghost sister, I am having trouble being a real person again. Dear ghost sister, my days have become a series of ritual and rearrangement. Dear ghost sister, the owls are out. Dear ghost sister, it's the moon and the stars provoking me, I am running in circles, naked in the dark. Dear ghost sister, touch me—catch me, hold me, unbury me. Dear ghost sister, let's live within each other's bones. Dear ghost sister, the apples will always fall, won't they? I am waiting for their echo, I am waiting for the storm. Dear ghost sister, the chair is empty, the chair and the wine glass and the mailbox and the picture frame. Dear ghost sister, remind me, again—which star is it that lies to the right of your ribcage? Dear ghost sister, are you holding your breath? Dear ghost sister, another flower petal. Dear ghost sister, another tumbleweed. Dear ghost sister, I've braided the sweetgrass, I've burned the sage, I've counted the radishes and the potatoes, I've dried the lavender and rosemary, I've stuffed the pillows with feathers and sewn them shut. Dear ghost sister, there's oil on the back of my neck. Dear ghost sister, I wrote *owl* when I meant to write *oil*—do you feel her? Dear ghost sister, I'm writing your name. Dear ghost sister, there's dust in my pocket that used to be a flower. Dear ghost sister, what is our real obsession—is it love or is it light? Dear ghost sister, there are rocks on the windowsill, seashells hanging across the glass. Dear ghost sister, I cannot thread the needle. Dear ghost sister, there is dirt on my tongue. Dear ghost sister, my energy is unpredictable, I am too many feet in one shoe. Dear ghost sister, my New Year's resolution was to feed myself. Dear ghost sister, are you still pulling out your hair? Dear ghost sister, the moonlight is dizzying. Dear ghost sister, I've hung the clothes to dry. Dear ghost sister, the shadow is cast by the constellation. Dear ghost sister, we are both haunted by dead women; it's their season; and mine, she is always returning, tugging at my shoulder from just below the surface of my skin. Dear ghost sister, I am untying all the knots; the full moon, the harvest, is rising and it has been five years since she ate her last plum. Dear ghost sister, the buttons are loosening from my shirt, socks are wearing thin, your ring slips from my finger down the drain. Dear ghost sister, there is blood on the napkin. Dear ghost sister, there is blood on the sink. Dear ghost sister, she follows me, her footsteps echo in the hall and I am afraid of looking in the mirror. Dear ghost sister, am I tethered to death or afraid of it? Dear ghost sister, ice melts into forgiveness. Dear ghost sister, another word for *life* is *afloat*.

THE RAGE DIARIES: NATURAL DISASTERS, ORIGINS

I. WAYS IN WHICH SHE IS AN AVALANCHE
Take care to pay attention to what is frozen on the inside.
Take care to pay attention to when it is melting.

> Let's talk about the ice queen.
> Let's talk about growing up in the snow.

The girl grown to woman in a colder landscape, a landscape covered in white, in ice, the gray afternoon she was pulled in a pink sled down the hill, the sled her mother was pulling, the sled that flipped over, the shock of her bare face hitting the sharp cold of the snow. It was almost warm. It pricked. She prickled. She could picture her cheeks: *rosy*. And her mother stood laughing because her reaction to the shock of the cold must have been funny, her mother stood laughing as her poor face froze.

Picture the top bunk close to the sagging ceiling. Picture the apartment with no living room furniture, only a table in the corner and a bare carpeted floor. She used to sleep covered in quilts, no heat in the room, no heat anywhere in the house except from the fake fireplace, except the unbearable space heater in the bathroom, where even the hot water in the shower ran cold after only a couple of minutes and she would shiver, naked before the frosted window—what did she look like, was her face red, would she have been any warmer if she had crawled into the snow?

She didn't know, so when she grew older, when she lived on her own, she did not want to pay for heat in the winter, stupidly letting her apartment get down to sixty, and then fifty, degrees. She never left the cabinet doors open—so what   if the pipes   could freeze? She slept in a cold bed upon a cold pillow, she wore a scarf and fingerless gloves and the thought of the cloth strangling her in her sleep didn't scare her, only the thought of leaving the space heater on for too long, forgetting to turn it off after she closed her eyes, she was not afraid of turning to ice she was only afraid of not waking up   before   she   burned.

She watched the snow falling from her window.
She watched it cover the top of her car and the sidewalk and the street
watched
as it came down in pockets, filling like ashes
like the crescent-moons of her fingernails she was (is) always
scattering about.

And she put the water on to boil.
And she put on another blanket.

And she buried herself   (she called it survival)   and she did
not let go.

II. WAYS IN WHICH SHE IS A TORNADO
is   it   only   because she spins?

When she's dancing sometimes she closes her eyes and loses herself to the sound and the motion the feeling of her hair as it whips around her head, as it tickles her neck. Sometimes she is the only one when she is dancing, not dancing alone but dancing by herself, oblivious to those around her, the bodies in motion, the bodies responding to the sound, she is dancing within her own funnel of movement, the paths she creates across the floor chaotic and unpredictable, she forces everyone else to be aware of her, to get out of her way. *Watch*. It is possible she will close her eyes and spin with abandon and straight into you. *Warning*. She is moving, a certainty, she is coming.

I cannot sit still for too many minutes
                    (except for the days when I cannot move).

I cannot remember some mornings what it feels like to dance, cannot remember the movement of muscles cannot fathom the journey across the room when I become frozen when I am the stillness when I am preparing for the storm to come.

Does a woman move differently   if she was a
girl in the Midwest?
The rustle of tall grass and knowledge of a prairie, the familiarity with flatness, with heavy air that can turn at any moment, clouds that can go black and angry in an afternoon, the stillness that promises wreckage— these are the conditions under which she grew arms and legs and hair and teeth and tits and fingernails. Her heart began beating in a part of the world that wrestles the wind, and the wind decides when it's time to come out to play, the wind moves on its own terms, the wind pulls the clouds into its rage and restlessness and need to move faster and larger and in a way that destroys and terrifies and reminds.

The wind wins.

And all is silent.
Except my mind.
Which keeps talking and talking though my body remains silent
(and still)

and I am no longer the tall grass I am no longer the flat earth, I am no longer the dancer, I am only the wind. Waiting. (*I am only the wind.*)

She spins, oh, she spins.

III. WAYS IN WHICH SHE IS A WILDFIRE

The burning ember the spark that falls upon dry grass the smoke that rises and covers the earth and fills the sky and tears through the atmosphere. She is the flame that grows into another, into another until the forest has fallen beneath her the trees the ash she rubs across her forehead and between her breasts, this past, what was, nothing but remnants of fire, of that which has been burned, she puts the heat of it upon her tongue and lets it melt her throat. She is fire, she could breathe it if she would only exhale, she could take this fucking stretch of the landscape down she could end it. She will walk out the back door and slam it behind her. She will not bother to lock it. She will leave you inside, exposed and vulnerable, she will make you take care of yourself, her hands will freeze in the cold but she will warm them with matches will warm them with breath, the flames of all that could have been words if she hadn't melted them into dust, she will leave you standing in a pool of gasoline and she won't flinch she will never look back.

She'll want to kiss a stranger to remember how it feels.
She could open her legs she could let them open, she could open them to let someone (come) inside.
She could be coming and she could be going she is going to rip holes in her tights she is going to shred them apart she is going to (come) she is going to lose her mind.
To remember how it feels.

And what, then, when she bursts into flames?
What then?
Just like the ashes from a cigarette   she   will   fall   down.

IV. WAYS IN WHICH SHE IS AN EARTHQUAKE

The plates are shifting. They are reaching toward one another beneath the ground. They are reaching, commingling, yearning; or they are pushing against, pushing into, slamming into, hitting, wanting to hurt.

And, oh, the things we do to each other when what we are wanting to do is   hurt.

Plates thrown against walls shatter, they crack when they fall to the floor, when they slip from the table when they are pushed from it, the yellow plate her grandmother gave her when she moved into her first apartment, the yellow plate that she dropped with a slice of pizza on it, that she sent off the table as she crashed into another room, as she stormed into the darkness to where she couldn't see, where she could not be seen, where she did not want to see anything and did not see the yellow plate she had loved as it was thrown into the trash, did not see the contents of the wineglass she had filled as they were poured down into the sink, she was in the darkness on the hardwood floor on the house's foundation on the dirt on the dirt on the dirt burying somewhere deep below it those plates.

Smashing.
Look at them: pressing into   each   other   hard.

Let's talk about what it is we are wanting to do when all we are wanting to do is hurt. It hurts when the earth breaks in half, hurts when the gap is a threat of what anyone could fall into, a gap going down into what is unfathomable, down into the fires, the furnace that heats us my god it is so warm it is so goddamned hot it is sweltering and she is melting, look, she is melting: into the floor her wineglass is empty and she doesn't know it yet and the sky is dark so she doesn't see it she is only attached to the floor (to the foundation to the ground, down   down   down) and is not thinking of what would happen if it   split.

Consider the plates as they press against each other, doing what they wish they could be doing, which, of course, is fucking. The plates have arms, don't they? The plates have lips and teeth and some have cunts and some have cocks and they get wet sometimes, they get hard, they want to reach for each other, for these most seductive parts. Whatever they are reaching for, the point is they are reaching, extending, bump-ing, vibrating, overlapping

(they only want to love)
(they only want to fuck)

they only want to fucking love

these plates, these plates they are crashing, cracking
and into the earth we all fall.

V. WAYS IN WHICH SHE IS A TIDAL WAVE

Just beyond some stillness there is the threat of sudden overflowing, water coming not as a relief but a roaring, an outpouring into a crash, a flood, the gradual (re)filling of every part.

The tide like the moon, like a woman, on a cycle—periodically she rises and she falls. The body of a woman a vessel; the body of the ocean an undulation; the shape a body of water curls into, roars into, breaks from; rising too high in a sudden onset of feeling, rising so high she must come crashing down, in a rush, this release her goodbye.

Goodbye to the houses goodbye to the trees goodbye to those left standing goodbye to the past and the roots and the dirt. She will fill all as she crashes, the holes and the alleys, and then she will fill some more, fill what is not meant to contain so much water, or any water, no more than a spill, no more than a puddle, because her body is swelling, she is dripping water from her pores it is falling from her fingertips it is soaking her hair, she is wet overflowing, she is roaring she is spilling she is careening toward the vessel, take it, take it all, all she can no longer hold. And the spaces she seeps into, the ground she soaks, the sky she mirrors—in vastness, in inescapability—the sky that she mirrors is holding its breath.

SELF PRACTICE

self-abasement self-absorption self-denial self-abuse self-removal self-analysis self-complacent self-assured self-betrayal self-assuming self-destructive self-conscious self-appointed self-serving self-imposing self-expression self-existent self-sufficient self-assessment self-hypnosis self-enjoyment self-judgment self-focused self-rising self-righteous self-determined self-aligning self-instructed self-loathing **SELF-DE-FINING** self-elected self-protection self-effacement self-storage self-generating self-igniting self-driven self-profit self-restraint self-reliant self-supported self-centered self-acting self-confessed self-confident self-evident **SELF-COMMITMENT** self-advancement self-destructive self-defeating self-cleaning **SELF-CONSUM-ING** self-consistent self-confinement self-caused self-winding self-repellent self-worship self-recording self-indulgent self-repression self-suggestion self-opinion self-loading self-seeking self-improvement self-importance self-healing self-created self-possessed self-devoted self-limited self-explanatory self-regard self-control self-prepared self-mastery self-prescribed self-dependent self-protection self-driven self-resentment self-applied self-regulating self-delight self-portrait self-restriction self-betrayal self-punishment self-respect self-defining self-winding self-assessment self-sown self-calibrated self-generated self-medicated self-fulfilling self-scrutiny self-pity self-storage self-dejection self-seeking self-starter self-torment self-righteous self-educated self-help self-suggestion self-reflection self-diagnosed self-sufficient self-instructed self-deprecating self-hood self-hypnosis self-mortification self-incriminating self-inflicted self-indulgent self-perpetuating self-murder self-profit self-initiative self-sustaining self-sabotage self-repellent self-evident self-moving self-repression self-professed self-sustaining **SELF-PORTRAIT** self-resentment self-imposed self-produced self-repair self-sustaining self-explanatory self-fulfillment self-resistance self-same self-pity self-doubt self-starter self-distrusting self-correcting **SELF-SURRENDER** self-improvement self-diagnosis self-interest self-induced self-torment self-insurance self-adjusted self-amputation self-consistent self-governed self-worship **SELF-REFLECTION** self-calibrating self-directing self-mastery self-trust self-prescribed **SELF-LOSS** self-mutilation self-annihilation self-mortification self-renunciation self-glorification self-dedication self-degradation self-inflation self-preparation self-accused self-examination self-love self-appreciation self-delusion self-congratulation **SELF-SACRIFICE** self-assigned self-proclaimed self-flagellation self-judgement self-manipulate self-repellent self-control self-driven self-fed **SELF-RISING** self-directed self-loathing self-protection self-governed self-improvement self-interest self-resentment self-enjoyment self-medicate self-serving self-forgetting self-praise self-employed self-profit **SELF-ALIGNING** self-assured self-collecting self-abandonment self-conceit self-approval self-consistent self-critical self-defeating self-delusion self-doubt self-made self-abuse self-composed self-applause self-regulating self-questioning self-execution self-pity self-important self-restoring self-flattery self-ignited self-inflicted self-correcting self-limited self-starter self-degradation self-evacuation self-addressed self-conscious self-delusion self-appreciation self-aware self-consuming self-analysis self-enrichment self-giving self-recording self-restraint self-indulgent self-suggestion self-development self-enamored self-judgement self-protection self-defining self-surrender self-taught self-worship self-same **SELF-LESS** self-neglect self-preoccupations self-torment self-abasement self-professed self-possessed self-trust self-loathing self-instructed self-examination self-hypnosis self-realization self-focused self-reflection self-styled self-reliant self-love self-loading **SELF-HELP** self-destroying self-sown self-advancement self-aware self-determined self-sustaining self-initiate self-operate self-accused self-discipline self-mastery self-prescribed self-approval self-confidence self-absorption self-aligning self-assessment self-glori-

fying self-propelled self-murder self-expression self-induced self-justifi-
cation self-portrait self-righteous self-explanatory self-applauding self-
caused self-certain self-denial self-sacrifice self-accused self-contained
self-moving self-devotion self-reproach self-perpetuating self-serving
self-insurance self-inflicted self-ward self-scrutiny self-transformation
self-imposed self-improvement self-named self-correcting self-mortification self-defined self-limited self-trust self-resentment self-generated self-worth self-execution self-hood self-diagnosis self-punishment
self-return self-incriminating self-deception self-opinion self-doomed
self-distrusting self-igniting self-evident self-death self-neglect
self-winding self-start self-sufficient self-pleasure self-abundance
self-cleaning self-indulgent self-involved self-commitment self-care-
self-fulfilling self-check self-abasement self-denial self-important
self-published self-recovery self-mockery self-certainty self-governed self-division self-struggle self-help self-manifestation self-driv-
ing self-creation self-seeking self-hate self-obsessed self-doomed
SELF-ERASURE the self will decide in time a self-icide.

(but not tonight.)

COVEN

CAST OF CHARACTERS

SYLVIA (thirty, poetess, ghost)

DIANE (actress, blonde, possibly depressed, possibly asleep; also known as Betty, possibly in a dream)

AUDREY (trapped in or after a coma, dances when the music is too dreamy)

LAURA (could have been someone else but instead is a dead girl)

SCENE: The other side of the mirror. SYLVIA, DIANE, AUDREY, and LAURA are peering out. The space behind them appears just as the space beyond them: there is furniture, an armchair, a bookcase, a desk, a couch; a rug on a hardwood floor, a lamp in the corner, a painting over the mantel. They move around as they speak, in phases, as if in rotation: one sits, then stands, rests against the bookcase; another follows; it is natural, rhythmic, hypnotizing.

SYLVIA: What follows in an explanation.

AUDREY: A dance.   DIANE: An illusion.   LAURA: A secret.
DIANE: A dream.

SYLVIA: The secret of forgetting. The illusion of reflection. The dream of avoidance, the dance of dying. She is watching.

LAURA: What is her name?

SYLVIA: Ghost.

DIANE: A ghost.   LAURA: A ghost.   AUDREY: A ghost.

SYLVIA: A communion.

LAURA: What is the dream, what am I waking from, what is the dream if I am not asleep?

AUDREY: What am I waking from?

DIANE: What is her name?

AUDREY: What is the dream?

LAURA: The last time a man put his cock in my mouth I could smell the ocean and taste smoke.

AUDREY: A warning.

LAURA: I could feel him go soft. I could feel my blood stop.

DIANE: A nightmare.

LAURA: My blood stopped and I was too close to the water to feel it too close to tomorrow to touch it too early and too late and too coked up to cry and too sad to scream and too dead to breathe too dead to speak too dead to smell the blood or taste the water or feel the chill too dead too dead too dead to have anything other than my name.

DIANE: A becoming.

SYLVIA: A piece of art.

LAURA (*loudly, urgently, frightened*): And the owls take flight and she bleeds with the new moon and she bleeds in the water and the water goes red and the fire goes out and the morning comes and the body is gone and the owl is gone and the moon is gone and the blood is everywhere and she is gone she is gone she is nowhere she is gone—

DIANE (whispers): Everything good was a dream.

LAURA: Wrapped in plastic.

SYLVIA: And the moon grows full. And her hair goes red.

DIANE: Trembling fingers, another drink, nipples hard on the glass—

                                                      LAURA: The window.

SYLVIA: And the flames turn to ash.

DIANE: I dream of her cunt.

AUDREY: Cavernous. LAURA: Blooming. SYLVIA: Red.

DIANE: I memorized every line and I looked at her on every cue and I made her cum to the climax of every song and I made her smile, made her impossible lips smile, I swear she was the devil her lipstick never came off.

    LAURA: A stain. AUDREY: A miracle. SYLVIA: Holy.

                        AUDREY: What is the dream?

              LAURA (*whispers*): I'll die again tomorrow.

SYLVIA: Dead for half a century.

    DIANE: I'll die tomorrow. AUDREY: Is this the dream?
    DIANE: If I'm not already dead.

SYLVIA: Under the right conditions—the weather and the remaining number of cigarettes and the poems finished and the coffee run out and the moon slipped from fullness and the moon slipped from vision—under the right conditions—

AUDREY: My clawing memory, the room filled with smoke and boom and then the room with the walls painted white, the man I don't love, the father and the son and the man who keeps me, the song still playing in my head, the one song that plays like a dream or the memory of it, and I know I must dance.

SYLVIA: Under the right conditions—the children asleep and the husband disappeared, the bird long ago left dead in the box.

              DIANE (*whispers*): I'll be dead tomorrow.

SYLVIA: Under the right conditions—

                      AUDREY: Dead or dreaming.

SYLVIA: Already a ghost.

        LAURA: Looking out from the other side of the mirror.

SYLVIA: She sees us.

                    AUDREY: Is she dreaming?

SYLVIA: Under the right conditions—

DIANE: Everything was an illusion.

AUDREY: The other side of the mirror…

DIANE: She's watching.

(PAUSE)

AUDREY: Is she dreaming?

LAURA: Where does a self go when no one else is in the room to see her?

DIANE: I keep forgetting—who is screaming when I am asleep?

SYLVIA: A ghost.

AUDREY: Where does she go?

DIANE: (*whispers*): The face in the mirror, where did she go?

SYLVIA: She is only a love letter.

AUDREY: The mirror reflects when no one is looking at it.

DIANE: The mirror reflects the faces I see in my dreams.

SYLVIA: She is both herself and lost in her own darkness.

LAURA: Her hair is red.   AUDREY: Her eyes are blue.
DIANE: Her skin is pale.

SYLVIA: Just a ghost, fogging the glass. (*exhales*)

DIANE: I ignore what is wrong with me in hopes it will kill me.

AUDREY: I pace the room, waiting to die.

DIANE: I'll be dead tomorrow.

LAURA: I'm already dead—I used to be.

SYLVIA: We exist on the other side. We are always looking out.

AUDREY: The most unnatural experience is seeing your own reflection. I see myself and I want to scream.

DIANE: Who is she?

AUDREY: I see myself and I want to scream.

DIANE: Who am I? Who is she? Which one of us is the dream?

LAURA: She lives outside the glass.   AUDREY: She still exists beyond the frame.

DIANE: She is awake after the dream.

SYLVIA: We are not dreaming and she is not dreaming she is one side and we are the other she is the glowing half of the moon and we are the blackness, the memory, the echo. We are already gone but she can hear the echo.

DIANE: I'll be dead tomorrow. AUDREY: If I'm not already.

LAURA: We are already. DIANE: We are ready.

SYLVIA: She wants to be ready. She is looking for us. She is looking for a face that looks familiar. She is wondering why every reflection looks like someone she's seen before, a person she knows. She is going to scream.

(LAURA screams.) (DIANE screams.) (AUDREY screams.)

SYLVIA: And the moon is full and the bed is empty and her candles are new, they won't burn forever, a candle burning, the moon in its phases, echoes of the hourglass, time running out. Tomorrow, tomorrow, a change in tone. The fire burned out, the moon does not glow, ashes and burned wax and red hair swept under the rug and her blood on the carpet her blood on tile her blood in the mirror, waking, walking, her blood, moving, still, into the night, her hair red and the fire burned out. Her red hair. A change in tone.

AUDREY: There is no one else.

SYLVIA: So no one will know she was too tired, bury it, bury the words and her heart and the moon, drag fallen boughs across the dirt to cover the secret she didn't want to be found.

DIANE: Whose secret?

AUDREY: Mine. LAURA: Mine.

SYLVIA. Hers. And mine. Mine is the mind she slips into at night when she lies in bed and thinks she is still asleep, she inhabits a ghost, she is a ghost.

LAURA: Unburied. AUDREY: Trapped. DIANE: Forgotten.
SYLVIA: Alone.

(The women pause. They are now standing in one line, side-by-side, close enough to be holding hands, but they are not. They are staring out of the mirror as it continues to hang. The glass appears to be cracking, the women grow distorted. Everything goes black. There is a scream.)

END SCENE

REFLECTION

WHAT EVER HAPPENED TO HER?

It was the fever, the great hot light behind her eyes, the glow that emanated upward and out from her chest, the very drum of her, the steady pulse turned to eruption turned to overflow. The heart cannot break when it is still burning, the flame enough to keep a body upright, keeps a mind up at night, flushes the face red to distract the chest from the encroaching blackness, the pit of sorrow, to coming ache. *I cannot sleep without these pills*, she said, *I cannot eat, there is no room, only heat inside of me, only light*. The product of mania is hot to the touch, the absorption dizzying: the chaos of circumstance, the

WHATEVER HAPPENED TO HER,

She trusted the narrative: blood flows through the body like a river, is never the same blood twice. She believed her body, still, to be capable of purity. Not even these eyes, she knew, could penetrate the darkness. She wanted to be more shadow than woman—tethered, spacious, elusive. When she made her own chest flush red in bursts of lust she didn't want anyone else to see it, her skin, she wanted to be the only one looking into and back at herself from the mirror, pulsing heart and shoulders rising to fall, watch the rash burn blood-like in strange continents before it faded and her skin returned to

33

madness of reaction, the anger, driving, the fever and its rage, the fever, it raged, until it was over. She was looking for that warmth again, looking for light. She was trying to be someone other than the self she was starting to believe she'd never been, hadn't yet been, *I haven't been anyone without him, haven't been anyone yet.* She was (heart)broke(n) and cold and awake in London, *I am not capable of being or loving myself.* What happened was the fever; it wasn't a dream. 103°, *but my body is colder, twenty pounds lighter, my love is gone.* The past a demon to be exorcised, write it up in a rhyme scheme, drench it with blood, let the ghost of it walk the halls and rattle the windows, trap it in a closet, hold it in your hand, try to remember all of the hands as they were when they were still living, when we were still living, *when I was still living*; get it out now before we are dead. The thermometer is broken. There must be an explanation: temperature up again, to 103°, no one believes her, she's still awake, her face isn't so red, and maybe it's the sun, she believes he hates her son, the candle will burn and she'll burn until the matches run out. An obsession: his echo, footsteps running through her veins, the death of their love still beating in her heart—cold now, empty, lights out. There is a difference between good and goodwill, and if goodness is willing there will be some

white. She never looked backward. She knew death was looking back. In a race against time she knew the only winner would be the one willing to stop looking at the clock, to tear up the calendar, to see the hours of both light and dark as a continuation of the other rather than each day as a beginning and each night, an end. Hours grow irrelevant as they continue stretching onward, and the more time that passed as she stayed in bed unmoving, the more life itself began to feel coffinlike, stifling. She burned candles from both ends so she could no longer measure what had been melted, instead becoming a magnificent pool of wax, flowing beyond the glass and glazing the surface of the windowsill, congealing like old sex on the carpet. How hard could it be to stop holding her breath? A radical ambition: to permit her body to turn to sediment, to be the sludge of the river, to bleed blooms of red at the water's surface like the glow of fireworks, a great, hot shock in the sky. A wound in reality knowing she would not be nothing as long as there was still death to follow her, as long as there were pages of history to burn. She filled her belly with the foods that made her feel sickest, followed the great lump of it with enough coffee to make her heart explode. She stared out the window and imagined the desert, air dry enough to shatter, sand hot enough to burn her feet, good coming out of the split. Split lives, split lips, the evisceration, the limbs lucked out, the lines run dry, the fever burns out in a dry hiss, smoke smoldering from the ashes that fizzle and flicker and pop to a stop. Like killing a fly: I smash the one that's been buzz-bothering me with no consideration, no thought about death until one swift palm-press against the window and the fly falls swiftly down, oozing yellow, the candle it was drawn to still burning bright. I start to dream of having fevers—is the dream of a fever a fever dream? When I am awake I dream of diseases, imagine every ache a rupture, every blur blindness, every stray blister unable to mend, the end of skin wearing down into itself, swelling and bursting, leaking and peeling and expanding again. I hold a thermometer between my lips as I make the bed in the morning and read 97° but sometimes I am colder. I am thinking of her every time I wake up in the night, heart beats out of dreaming, the oven, *the heart of the house*, she kept it burning in their country home in the days growing closer to winter, kept the stove burning like he never could, the power of fever inside her, hot rage, mania's illumination. Nothing to gain when the night turns its lights out. Stars become candles, see how they burn. Get one near enough and lean toward the fire, take a deep breath, blow its flame out. Will the house

a climate her body did not know. She'd scratch her name in the soft, loose surface, watch what she'd believed once to be permanent disappear fast enough to feel certain she'd never been. She'd keep a candle burning, just one, from the top, in the center of the house, the heart of it, her heart at the altar, altered to pulse to the flicker of the glow, the internal flame no one else could blow out. *What a strange place*, she'd say, *what a strange girl*. All the hours that flowed into the wax and melted into more hours, all the days and the nights, the breaks from the light and the escape from the dark, she felt it was endless, this strange, endless world. She kept waiting for the next paragraph, kept waiting for the closing half of parentheses, the end of the interlude, kept waiting for her hands to grow strong enough for the handle, for the blade of the knife to grow sharp enough to finally carve straight through her insignificance. She collected small tokens, gathered rocks and feathers and bones and flowers and pieces of colorful glass. She dressed herself in tree bark and lined her eyes with dirt. She stayed awake all hours to convince herself her dreams weren't real. She covered the mirror with a sheet to try to forget herself. Voices attached, likely, to bodies, but she could no longer see anyone other than her self in the mirror, the self she was told belonged to her—was it even still have a heart when the body within its walls is dead? The echo of a self does not tap on the door, does not run the water, does not leave a dent or a muss in the bed. The self does not echo itself, she does believe in herself, does not know herself to be a self in this new house, burning sometimes the day's candle from both ends. She wanted to be luminescent, to glow from the inside, wanted to be bright enough to light the room for herself in the dark when he's sleeping, when he turns the lights out, when the house has gone cold and empty, when she is feeling her forehead each morning expecting the fever, praying for it to return, he will not return, they will not return to what they were and what they were was not who she should, could, would have been. Her temperature is not rising the way that it used to and she keeps waking in the cold house, her heart empty, she turns on the oven and kneels down before it, ready to return to that mania, the fever, the glorious hot white. Years earlier the shocks were administered to be the reversal. Turn backward, time, turn back to a sensation that this throat can swallow easier, turn back to a situation that these bones can comprehend. Electricity flowing through the veins, bright hot blood, sizzling, bright hot red turned to glowing white. *Wake up.* Without a pulse she's not sleeping, without a pulse that lifts a heart

her body, this self, or was it another, divided, the other half, peering back at her when she wasn't looking, was it her body or was it death, itself? At any volume a whisper, the breath of a tone that begs her come closer, seductive, sinister, urgent. She heard it from the walls of her heart and her house and the flame of the candle and the heat of the oven—*come closer*, she heard it in her bones and in the sky and in the mirror—*I want you.* Coming closer to what, wanted by whom? She scratched her arm until the skin broke, clipped her fingernails short and made her gums bleed. The voice said, *it's me, it's me, your madness.* She spoke back to herself, hush, caught up in the rhythm of blood rushing, the cadence of dripping water, caught beneath the sheet of hot desert sand, blowing over every trace of herself, the air too dry for the echo to disappear into, her mouth too dry even to speak. Giving in is no longer feeling the conditions of the atmosphere. Giving up is setting fire to the mailbox before the letters go out. She no longer slept through the night. Dreams woke her shivering and left her quite shaken: a black feather, a masked man, an act of violence, a maze, a mad dog, biting. Thoughts turned toward nonsense and away from reality, nothing quite clear in the dark of four-thirty, nothing quite clear in the ritual confusion of getting out of bed again to check the locks on toward a vision of possibility, a heart that pulses to a rhythm upbeat. Fumes of mania: breathe in. The days spent in exhaustion, she cannot sleep, not without pills, or brandy, she does not sleep. The fever meant to snap this brain toward a reversal, hot enough, bright enough, sweat out the hysterics, the sadness, the sin. Enough heat to sweat out the future—the past is all she can live for, and she's had enough. Enough of this body. These toes and these feet. These legs, these hips, this cunt, these nails, these bones. These hands and this heart. These arms. These shoulders. This chest, this belly, these tits, this ass. These veins. This blood. This blood and this body. This hair, these eyes, this nose, these ears, this mouth. This chin. These lips. This forehead. This fever. These lungs. These veins. This blood. This knife on the counter. This glass of wine. This glass, the whole bottle, this holy bottle, this holy body, this blood, this body of blood. This skin—break it. Slice, carve it open. Scratch the surface with these nails sharpened, these nails knifelike, scratch long and hard enough until the itch turns to wound. This wound. These wounds. They sit on this tongue and this throat swallows them, chokes the blood down. This blood. This body's own blood. This blood and this house and this oven and the knife. Hot and sharp. Electric and piercing the doors. She did not like to be awake in the dark and did not like to be asleep in it either—*if only I can will my eyes to stay open until the sky grows bright, if only*—she'd wake again to a sun-filled room and start again. Again. Again and she grew older. As moments in her memory that had once been vivid, present, slipped further, it occurred to her that there is no moment at which one starts growing older, no age at which the transition occurs, the only constancy to living another year/day/hour/minute is that a body continues to grow old. There is no space to start over, no year/day/hour/minute that turns over and backward and back in on itself—even the new light, even the dust swept, even without any clutter, bones get packed into boxes that crowd all the corners. Crowd like her thoughts: too many, and the only proper thing to do is close the door and seal the cracks. The continued contradiction: she'll wake to sleep and sleep to wake up, busying herself in between. One palm reads chaos and the other redemption. No tea leaf can predict her past as it haunts her, no tarot card can organize the constellation of spaces she hasn't been. She'll swallow until her throat stops hurting, keep filling up boxes until her year/day/hour/minute runs out, rest her bones in one corner and fill up another, let the dust collect around her and the lightbulb above burn ing. If this brain won't sleep through the night, this fire, this flame, this fog, this heat, this never-ending summer, this winter-scented house, this fever, this echo, comes back in the morning, come back to this morning and ask for the knife. This shock is not meant to harm, it's meant to make better; this fire not meant to engulf, but to keep warm; this knife meant to cut. This fever meant to make desperate and to delude. This body meant to carry blood, meant to let blood, this body meant to pour blood, this poor blood, this body meant to die—in which version, the truth or the mythology? These hands form the steeple, looking for the church, soaking up the blood like she'd soak up a spilled bottle of wine. Afterward, she felt much renewed. The fog had been lifted and the feathers on the birds outside no longer dried out. They called again prettily, the tit and the sparrow, the guinea, the starling. Each night star glowed brighter, each phase of the moon—tangible, a sliver to climb onto, a half-wafer to swallow, a whole bright bed, a full bed on which to finally sleep. Her eyes began to glow brighter, too, her skin cold with no fever to keep the blood warm. Most days feel like nonsense, but she's still awake. Awake to infinity, wanting to dream if only to be gone, to exit the body, to feel more celestial than blood, skin, and bones. A pre-out. Her feelings get hurt but nothing matters, will matter, it's all going to end. Whatever happens to her, she thinks, will be at a distance. Whether she swallows a piece of glass or a mountain there is nothing that can fill her nothing enough of a balm nothing but more to be swallowed and she will still swallow if only to prove she hasn't yet lost her breath. Whatever happens will be at a distance. All day again and then into tomorrow and until she is too old to keep her eyes from falling shut.

scription for sedative-hypnotics. Tossed over and under the shiny counter. Take enough and she won't have to wake up. Dull the body to disaster and manipulate the mind to distraction; dull the mind and manipulate the body. Trick the mind into believing it is composed of fragments that can be studied and magnified and loved and rejected at will; bend the body into a shape like sediment, no longer drifted but dropped to the bottom. Let the mind believe in the reflection it sees on the surface of the river. The river flows within, veins carrying blood like water, the constant roar of it, traveling downstream and up, circulating without thought but with rhythm—is blood, like water, never the same blood twice? She trusted the narrative: death is looking back. She turned on the oven to air the house out—the fumes of the heart that had once been her house made her woozy, she wanted to breathe, she wanted only to know steadiness again, to be still like water, standing water, the most stagnant kind, the ice in air so cold it will never grow slick again, never stick, never melt. Her blood was chirping, *free me*, but she couldn't find the spot to let it out; she stilled it, *hush*, not needing to be dead again, only risen, only needing to be free. No one was given any warning, not a call or a letter or a whisper or wink. She burned the mailbox before the letters went out, set fire to any trace of her echo—*does a corpse have a shadow?*—wanting to leave only her self, ignore the details. Not enough to dig into, not enough of a secret to tell. Her muscles itched at the opportunity to escape each time the echo returned, each time the deep hollow of her bones filled with water, rushing, blood like water, each time the clock turned to the four o'clock hour when it could have been morning but nothing outside was yet bright. Dread filled her lungs when she couldn't make out an exit. She wrote a letter, her warning, her elegy, folded the paper and placed it in an envelope, sealed the flap shut with her tongue, stamped and addressed it to herself, carried it to the mailbox and closed the door, raised the flag, doused the mailbox with gasoline and lit a match, threw it, turned on her heels back into the house, still only in the morning hours before morning. Her final words: still in mourning. The echo turned backward and back in on itself. She longed to be *a verb instead of an adjective*, committed herself to undertaking this choice, to achieving a state of being other than as a noun. Person, place, or thing: in motion, becoming, whirling, shivering, screaming, burning. Not to be ready but to ready herself, too ready, ready for the transition, ready, all ready, to go. She'll continue to let the mania marinate. No tea leaf can predict her past as it haunts her, no tarot card can organize the fate she's promised herself. She leaned into the knife too closely when it started to speak. She leaned in to hear it whisper, *I'm here*, she heard it, she and shuddered and turned on the gas. She didn't want to hear the knife speak anymore, wanted to close her eyes and drift away for a day or two, wanted to drift toward oblivion, on her knees, a violent prayer. Snow fell outside the window and icicles hung from the roof's edge, each one a sharp sliver, echoing the knife's song, *I stab, I stab*. The wind carried the voices through town and through the cracks in the old buildings, through the thin glass windows, through any door left open for even just a moment, a threat, a chorus: *I stab, I stab*. She wanted quiet. Her heartbeat kept interrupting the silence, the rhythm a mutation of history: *I am/not anymore*. A rosary could be no substitute for a noose. A heartbeat not violent enough to be a storm, not even when it pounds, not even when it is pounding, her heart pounding when she knelt down, her heart had once been a message, a secret, a reminder; her heart had once been when it was pounding. She broke the ice. Ended the conversation. In her dreams enough wax melted from the candles for her to lower herself into it. In her dreams there was a lightness, a stunning fight-or-flight-lessness. An internal blister popped and oozing by accident. A thirst she cannot quell, or doesn't, leaves the throat dry and slips a wick inside, strike a match and light herself up, let herself slip into the oblivion of beginning to melt.

TRAJECTORIES

I.

An unbecoming is only an unbecoming if one is becoming unable to be one's self, to come out of the bedroom, brush her teeth and wash her face and look out the window, look at that: again, there is the sun and it is shining; there is the sky and it is blue. As blue as the blood goes before it goes red, another mythology, that what is flowing within us like water is, like water, ever actually blue. We are red on the inside, and pulsing, and wet, we are wed to the functions we don't give permission to, that occur without warning or preparation, a continuation: where it is snowing and where it will snow. If a piece of paper is folded in half and in half again, torn into four separate parts, it is still paper but now in four pieces, four pages for turning, four stones to step onto, one to the other and then to the next and the next one. My art was origami because I wanted to fold my own birds to hang by delicate strands from the ceiling as if I could bring the sky closer, as if I could surround myself with feathers and blue. Every waking moment is an act of imagination: here I am and I am becoming; here I am and I am going to grow. No matter how deep we dive into mind-water, we'll never be the river, never be the bird, never the mountain, never the moon. I can close my eyes and my body is a body unbodied, but then if this were true I would not have eyes to close. I pick at the wound to prove it is healing; I'm bleeding, alive, this doesn't hurt, I am okay. Flowers are dying the moment they are pulled from the ground, aren't they, but they keep their color. The yanking doesn't matter, the severed roots, the dirtied water, the drooping petals, the decay. I keep dried flowers beside me like sheets of paper to walk upon, a tool. This doesn't hurt; I am okay.

II.

If anything hurts I have to fix it. A habit is an obsession is a ritual is a drug. The act of addiction: treat and repeat, repeat and repeat and repeat until better, repeat until satisfied, repeat until someone tells you the repetition is no longer healthy and then repeat the replacement until a station near normal is found. There are Normals all over this country, this country with a lack of identity, a no-place where trees fall and no one is bound; unlike books constructed to be held meticulously together, we are pages held together by staple, a swift tug and we are separated once again. I dream of a stranger who ties me to the bed and lights matches to throw at my naked skin. I dream of people I know I need to escape from. I dream of adrenaline: I fight and I fly and during the day my ritual is to feel, fill, freeze. Which was the wine-daze and which was the dream? I sort through the images, the blur of my being, wake with sweat on my chest and then the air hangs cold again. Histories are (re) covered, bones dug up, found, and if they must be recovered they must have once hurt—being discovered a fate that must have been wrong to begin with. What is wrong is to have lit matches thrown at your naked skin—but what do I need to recover from if the act occurred in a dream? Shake my head hard enough and the landscape will change, some severed memories I've locked up will fall out and I'll have to discover what's hurt me and how to be better all over again. Re-cover: sweep the dust back under the rug, lock up the evidence and put it out of sight, bury it, plant a tree or flowers to let another narrative grow.

III.

Normal becomes lost hours in the still-night of morning. Normal becomes the redundancy of the same four walls. Normalcy becomes forgetting the days and not speaking and no sex drive. Normalcy becomes the anxiety of another generation, another generation growing depressed. I sink into solitude, the acceptance of unbelieving, the new strangeness of my life. Normal becomes no longer making plans because what is the point of them and what do I want anyway, and anyway, my body is too old to dance the way I finally want to. Years of training lead nowhere when my mind hasn't yet translated the work into art. Years of drinking won't matter if I don't have any plans. A moment in time like a photograph is captured, something taken, something violently removed from the current, the true state of being, and I can be taken and trapped in a frame, hang me to the wall I don't feel real anyway.

A blankness crowds my mind every evening, a rush of terror: *this is all there is*. For me today, there will be the wet of desire: desire to escape, drift farther and more feather-like to some safe faraway. Instead of making plans I pick at my nails. Instead of trying something new I rely on patterns—the shape of my body traced in blue ink on the hardwood in a corpse pose. Yesterday's tomorrow is becoming another broken invitation, a housecoat smelling of some foggy sweetness, sweat or incense or berries or mushrooms. If I wait patiently enough for it, my mania will come, my magnificence, my thin, fraying line. I wait for a vision to come more clearly, a vision other than water and fire rushing over each last inch of earth.

IV.

Most lives are very simple. A life is lived until it is over, a body a landscape of days spent searching, attempting to map out a meaning for itself in the world, a meaning and a home. A body fixed within the space that surrounds it, surrounded by space on all sides, horizons and vistas and ocean and sky the echoes of flesh and bone and veins. A bruise blooms and fades but the pain of memory extends deeper. I wake up, I get up, I saturate the hours with worry until I can go back to sleep. I am tethered to past traumas, tattered by future chaos. Life wounds by definition: the trajectory of living is to experience; a life experience is what categorizes a body as a person that things have happened to; life generates the experience of both learning to live and wanting to die. Most lives are very simple. Most deaths are simple, too. The matter-of-factness of *is* and *is no longer*, such small words, entire generations *were* this and *are* that and can be accounted for like the hand is to the thumb. Even Sylvia Plath did not live spectacularly; it's the simplicity of a being relating simply to the cadence and shadow of another being, the framework for constructing another experience, conducting an existence, conforming to deliverance, as in *deliver me*, from nothing special and nothing spacious and I am another in a crowd of beings who hurt.

I assert every day is familiar, all days are each other until the day that is the end. I crumple up a piece of paper, the sound like cicadas or snowfall, any day is every day and today could be any season and if there is no reason then why am I hurting what am I hurting why are we hurting and where does it end?

With a bang. A bang or crash or perhaps just an exhale: the pain of removal is knowing the wound was there in the first place.

RESURRECTION

Her tarot deck is missing a card. She saw it in her sleep.
A woman on her back on a wooden cross in the grass.
She pulled it once. She pulled it a second time, reversed, and heard the
word *resurrection*.
Who was the girl in the grass on the card she pulled in her sleep?

> *The color was black and at once it was glowing. The outlines*
> *were orange and purple and green. Her hair*
> *reminiscent of wheat fields, her hair the fringe of a broom.*
> *Brittle. Frayed. Used.*
> *Her eyes were facing toward the sky, would be looking at it*
> *if they were open.*

*The card it was glowing the card that she pulled the card the same color as the
world she pulled it in the dream world the blackorangepurplegreen world the
goddamned unreachable world but what if she could reach it could she reach it
could she reach her hand into the clouds and pull out this card put her fingertips
onto the sleeping (dead) woman's eyelids pull them open stare into the brilliance
of them the emptiness of them the absolute unknown blackorangepurplegreen of
them would they be visible would they look back at her would they glow would*

the woman on the card blink back at her look back at her and would her lips purse would her jaw begin to unhinge would she stretch her arms beyond the frame and whisper the word:

free.

NOTES:

"YET THE PHANTOM WAS PART OF THE FLOWER": The title is borrowed from a line in *The Waves* by Virginia Woolf.

The following italicized lines, in conversation with my own, are borrowed:

Sanity is found at the centre of convulsion, where madness is scorched from the bisected soul. (Sarah Kane "4.48 Psychosis") (Kane, Sarah. *Complete Plays.* London: Methuen Publishing Ltd, 2001.)

Illusion shapes and shelters us, as necessary as oxygen and water. Illusions won't die, they are not delusions, and seem part of a human being's hard-wiring. (Lynne Tillman, *Men and Apparitions*) (Tillman, Lynne. *Men and Apparitions.* New York: Soft Skull Press, 2018.)

You are not dead, although you were dead. The girl who died. And was resurrected. Children. Witches. Magic. Symbols. Remember the illogic of fantasy. (*The Unabridged Journals of Sylvia Plath*) (Plath, Sylvia. *The Unabridged Journals of Sylvia Plath.* Ed. Karen V. Kukil. New York: First Anchor Books, 2000.)

"llorando por tu amor" are lyrics from the song "Llorando" as performed by Rebekah del Rio in "Mullholland Drive."

"THE KNIFE SPEAKS": *This dark thing that sleeps in me, I know the bottom,* and *how you lie and cry after it* are all borrowed from "Elm" by Sylvia Plath; *I guess you could say I've a call* is borrowed from "Lady Lazarus" by Sylvia Plath; *oh, you strange girl* is borrowed from *The Unabridged Journals of Sylvia Plath*.

(Plath, Sylvia. *Ariel.* New York: HarperPerennial Modern Classics, 2018.)

(Plath, Sylvia. *The Unabridged Journals of Sylvia Plath.* Ed. Karen V. Kukil. New York: First Anchor Books, 2000.)

"COVEN": Diane, Audrey, and Laura are the names of characters created by David Lynch. My characters are meant to be inspired by these characters as I imagine them in conversation with Sylvia Plath. Elements of the conversation/details within the language are inspired by "Twin Peaks" and "Mulholland Drive."

"REFLECTION": The following lines in Italics are from *The Letters of Sylvia Plath Volume 2*, whether fully quoted or creatively interpreted/expanded upon: *I haven't been anyone without him, haven't been anyone yet*; *I am not capable of being or loving myself*; *the heart of the house*; *a verb instead of an adjective*. (Plath, Sylvia. *The Letters of Sylvia Plath Volume 2: 1956-1963*. Edited by Peter K. Steinberg and Karen V. Kukil. New York: Harper, 2018.)

ACKNOWLEDGMENTS

Thank you to the editors of the following journals, where versions of these essays first appeared:

"Yet the Phantom Was Part of the Flower," *Miracle Monocle*, Issue 19, 2022

"The Knife Speaks," *Grimoire Magazine*, Issue 10 "The Goth Narcissus," 2022

"The Rage Diaries," *Grimoire Magazine*, Issue 11, "Medusa: Stone Cold Bitches," 2023

"Reflection," *Fence*, Issue 40, 2023

"Trajectories," *Birdcoat Quarterly*, Issue 13, 2023

Thank you to my ghost sister and creative partner, Emma, for so much love and light.

Thank you to my brother, Landon, for always trying to understand.

Thank you to my parents for the roots.

Thank you to Tess and Caitlin and Megan for being the women you are—constant, brilliant, unwavering pillars, each in your own magnificent way.

Thank you to the spectacular team at Split/Lip for believing in my work and handling every part of the process of publication with such care.

Thank you to all those who support and have supported me in ways big or small—I am endlessly grateful to be surrounded by such good hearts.

HEATHER BARTEL is founder and co-editor of the literary journal and community, *The Champagne Room*. Her work can be found in *MAYDAY*, *Fence*, *Heavy Feather Review*, *Grimoire*, *Miracle Monocle*, *Leavings*, *Birdcoat Quarterly*, and elsewhere. She lives in Columbia, MO.

NOW AVAILABLE FROM
SPLIT/LIP PRESS

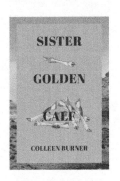

For more info about the press and titles,
visit us at www.splitlippress.com

Follow us on Instagram and Twitter: @splitlippress

Made in the USA
Monee, IL
06 May 2024

57849088R00038